By Dina Anastasio
Illustrated by Tom Barrett

Modern Curriculum Press
Parsippany, New Jersey

Cover and book design by Lisa Ann Arcuri

Modern Curriculum Press
An imprint of Pearson Learning
299 Jefferson Road, P.O. Box 480
Parsippany, NJ 07054–0480

www.pearsonlearning.com

1-800-321-3106

ISBN: 0-7652-2159-4

1 2 3 4 5 6 7 8 9 10 11   MA   07 06 05 04 03 02 01 00

Contents

For Eliza and Isabella,
with love

CHAPTER 1

Landing on Beta

Kiki was sleeping when the spaceship lurched and slowed. She opened her eyes and peered through the window. It was light outside. She glanced at her watch and saw that it read 9:00 A.M. She wondered where they were. They must be close to a star, but from what she could see outside, the light wasn't coming from Earth's sun.

"Are we home yet?" Carlos asked. He was sitting in the seat beside his friend. Carlos had been sleeping, too. "This place doesn't look like our solar system," Carlos said, as he leaned closer to the window. "That star is not our sun."

"No, it isn't," Kiki sighed. She was looking forward to getting back to Earth. She had been gone for a long time. Her father sometimes took her with him on business trips during school vacations. This time he had wanted her to see some of the Alpha Galaxy, which was a long way from the Milky Way Galaxy, where the Earth was a tiny planet among millions of stars. He had even let Kiki invite her friend Carlos to join them.

Everything they had seen had been fun and interesting. Now the winter vacation was almost over, and she was ready to go home. She wanted to get home in time to celebrate the new year with the rest of her family and friends.

Kiki glanced at her watch again. "The captain said we wouldn't get home to Earth until tomorrow morning," she said. "Did you feel the ship jerk?"

"I felt it all right," Carlos said. "Do you think something's happened to the ship?"

The spaceship lurched again. Then the captain's voice crackled through the speaker.

"This is Captain Brown," he said. "We need a new part for our ship. We'll have to make a stop on the planet Beta."

"Wow! We're going to land," Kiki said.

"Beta is a friendly place. It's a well-known stop in the Alpha Galaxy," the captain went on. "We have called ahead and found out that their flight center has the right part for our ship. Don't worry. We'll be back on Earth in plenty of time to ring in the year 2500. Since we'll be on Beta for a few hours, feel free to get off the ship for a while. If you haven't been here before and you're from Earth, you will need to wear gravity boots. Beta is a much smaller planet than Earth is, so there is less gravity here. The gravity on Beta has about the same pulling force as Earth's moon. The boots will help you keep your feet on the ground."

As Captain Brown prepared to land the spaceship, Kiki's father reminded her and Carlos to put their gravity boots on over their shoes and buckle their seat belts. It wasn't long before they landed. Kiki and Carlos headed for the door.

When they got outside, Kiki pointed up to the sky and said, "Look, Carlos, Beta has two suns. We could only see one from inside the spaceship. Two suns are really different from Earth where there's only one. According to my watch it's almost 9:30 A.M."

"Your watch is on ship time," Carlos said. "We don't know what time it is on Beta. We don't even know how long the days are. I wonder what kind of life there is here." He sounded very excited and a little bit nervous.

"We must be able to communicate with the creatures who live here," Kiki told him. "Captain Brown said they had the right part for the ship. I wonder what they look like."

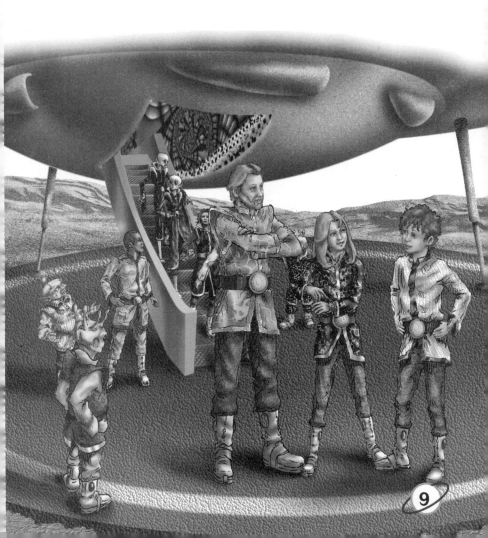

Kiki loved to travel to other planets because everyone looked so different. On one planet she had been to, there was so much water that the creatures who lived there had fins. No one had feet because there was no place to walk. On another planet, everyone had tiny little eyes. It was too dark to see much, so they didn't need to use their eyes to know where they were going. Instead they used their ears and noses to sense what was around them.

Everyone gathered together on the landing strip. Some people started asking Captain Brown to tell them a little about Beta. Kiki and Carlos walked over to the group to listen.

Before Captain Brown had a chance to talk, a strange little air-powered vehicle slid across the landing strip and stopped near him. Something handed a box to the captain. Kiki and Carlos couldn't tell what the pilot looked like. It was dressed in a thick white suit and a helmet and its bottom half was inside the vehicle.

Kiki was trying to see what was inside the vehicle when she heard a sudden, loud, banging noise in the distance. She jumped.

"Did you hear that?" Carlos whispered.

"Yes," Kiki said. "I wonder what's going on."

The noise was getting louder and more rhythmic. It sounded like hundreds of drums were booming. Added to the noise were blasts that sounded like trumpets.

"I think I hear people shouting, too," Kiki said. "It sounds close, maybe just over there." Kiki pointed toward a hill.

Kiki walked over to her father. "Dad, do you know what that noise is?" she asked. "It's coming from the other side of that hill."

"No, I don't," her father said. "Captain Brown said something about this being a big day on Beta, but he didn't get a chance to explain. He had to take the ship part to his crew."

"Can we climb up that hill and take a look?" Kiki asked.

"All right," her father said, "but don't stay too long or go too far. Captain Brown said we have to leave by nightfall at the latest."

Kiki looked at her watch again. It said 9:35 A.M. She thought they would have plenty of time to find out what the noise was. She had forgotten what Carlos had said about Beta time.

"Dad, could you ask Captain Brown to send some kind of a signal before the ship is ready to go?" Kiki asked.

"I'm sure he'll do something to let everyone know they have to get back on the ship," her father said.

"OK. Come on, Carlos," she said. "Let's go look." Carlos and Kiki ran for the hill. It didn't take them long to get to the top.

CHAPTER 2
The Games Begin

At the top of the hill, thick bushes blocked their view. Kiki and Carlos couldn't see anything, although the noise was now nearly deafening.

"Those drums are really loud now," Carlos said. "Whoever is making that noise must be on the other side of these bushes. Maybe we should turn back."

"I just have to see what's going on," Kiki said. "Look, there's a little gap in the bushes. Let's go."

Carlos and Kiki began to squeeze through the bushes. After a couple of steps, Kiki began to feel a little scared. The leaves seemed to cling to her shirt and hair like sticky tape or little hands. They rattled together and made a terrible clacking sound. These bushes were definitely not like Earth plants.

Finally, Carlos and Kiki pulled themselves out from the bushes on the other side. "I don't think I want to go back that way," said Kiki.

"Yeah," said Carlos, panting. "Those leaves are really strange."

Carlos and Kiki were standing on a hillside looking down at what appeared to be a large arena. The drums and trumpets were quiet now. Someone was shouting.

"Listen," Kiki whispered, "can you understand what language that is?" Carlos shook his head no.

Kiki turned a small knob on her watch. Now the voice was speaking English through a small speaker.

"Turn on your translator," she told Carlos. He turned the same knob on his watch.

"It sounds like an announcement," Carlos said. "The announcer is saying something about a schedule of events."

The voice said, "Welcome to the one thousandth Alpha Galaxy Games. Today's events will be for all two-legged, two-armed contestants from the Alpha Galaxy. The first event is the high jump, followed by the ball toss, then the long jump. The last event is the 100-yard dash. All teams take your places, please."

"It's the Alpha Galaxy Games!" Kiki cried. "I've read about them. A lot of people call them the Aggies after the first letter in each word. You know, AGG? They're a lot like the Olympic Games on Earth. Teams compete from all the planets in the Alpha Galaxy."

They slid down the hillside until they were close enough to see what was going on. Then they sat down, hoping no one would spot them.

Creatures of all shapes and sizes were huddled in groups on an open field. They seemed to be warming up. Some were jumping up and down, and some were stretching.

"I've never seen so many different kinds of people!" Carlos gasped. "Each team has a different uniform. The contestants with striped shirts look a lot like us except they're all very tall."

"The players with checked uniforms have big ears, like elephants," Kiki said.

"Look at the contestants in the uniforms with dots! Their eyes are on the sides of their heads, like hammerhead sharks," Carlos said.

Suddenly, one member of each team moved toward a circle in the middle of the field. It was time for the first event, the high jump, to begin.

As the contestants were lining up, Kiki noticed something. She leaned over to Carlos and said, "I don't think anyone is wearing gravity boots."

"I guess they don't need them," Carlos said. "They're probably used to moving around in weaker gravity. I've heard that most of the earthlike planets in the Alpha Galaxy are smaller than Earth, so the pull of gravity isn't as strong. Can you imagine what would happen if we took off our heavy boots?"

"We'd bounce about ten feet up in the air with every step," Kiki laughed.

"Think what would happen if we tried to jump without our boots. We'd probably go 30 feet up in the air, then just float down," Carlos said.

Carlos looked over at Kiki and saw that she was frowning. He knew that meant she was thinking hard. He knew what she was thinking about because he was thinking the same thing.

"I wonder what you have to do to join in the games," Kiki said. "I wonder if they'd let us."

"That wouldn't be fair," Carlos said. "Without our boots we'd be sure to win. We'd be able to jump higher than anyone else.

"Carlos, I have never won anything. This could be my big chance to do something great," Kiki said.

"We don't belong to any of those teams, and we're not from the Alpha Galaxy. Don't forget we have to get back to the ship," Carlos said.

"Shhh," Kiki said as she pointed toward the arena. "The announcer is saying something."

"Hi! How high can you jump?" the announcer said.
"We've got some cool rules. They're not school rules
or fool rules or pool rules. These are the high jump
rules. One member of each team will compete in the
high jump. One at a time, contestants will try to jump
over the bar. If you hit the bar or jump under the bar,
you're out. If you clear the bar, you may try again and
again until you miss. The bar will be raised after all
contestants complete a jump. OK, let's play."

"I can win the high jump," Kiki told Carlos.

"You'll get in trouble," Carlos said.

"No, it'll be easy," Kiki went on. "I'll keep my boots on at first. Then when I take them off I'll fly over that bar. I'll win it for sure." Carlos shook his head.

Kiki ignored him. "I've even got the right shirt," she said. "I've got squiggles, and no one else has squiggles. There are so many people on the field, no one will know I'm not one of the contestants."

"Wait!" Carlos cried as Kiki ran to the arena. He couldn't believe she was going down there. He followed, trying not to be noticed by anyone.

CHAPTER 3
Making the High Jump

Kiki stood in the line for the high jump and waited. No one noticed her or said anything because there were so many contestants. On her first jump she cleared the bar easily, but so did everyone else.

Somebody raised the bar. Kiki cleared it again, but this time two people missed. Two more people missed on the third jump. Kiki cleared it, but it wasn't easy.

It was time to take off the gravity boots. Kiki ran over to the bushes by the side of the field and untied them. As soon as they were off her feet she felt very light in her thin shoes and socks. She had to be careful not to step down too hard and bounce too high.

As she practiced walking before going back onto the field, she looked up. She noticed that the two suns were now in a different part of the sky. When she and Carlos had first left the ship, the suns had been directly overhead. Now they were lower. She looked at her watch again. Still, it was only a little past 10 A.M.

Kiki decided that she'd better start thinking about how to win the high jump and not worry about anything else. She had plenty of time.

"There is very little gravity on this planet," she said to herself. "I can win this event with no trouble at all."

Still, what if she flew too high? She would need something to hold her down.

Kiki found a rock that was just the right weight. She put it under her shirt. Then she pulled up the ends of her shirt and tied them around the rock. The rock was perfect. She didn't bounce when she stepped down as long as she was careful.

Kiki made her jump. She cleared the bar with an inch to spare, and no one guessed that she was an Earthling. Everyone else missed the highest bar, and she was declared the winner.

She raised her arms above her head. The crowd cheered and hollered.

"Tell us the name of your dream team," the announcer shouted over the noise of the crowd. "Tell us the name of your extreme team. Tell us."

Kiki quickly made up the name of a planet. "We are from the far, far planet Zera on the other side of the Alpha Galaxy," she shouted back. There was a moment of silence as the announcer tried to find the name Zera on the list of teams. He started to ask, "Where . . . .?" Then the crowd started cheering loudly again, and the question was forgotten.

Before she went to get her award, she walked over to the bushes and put her gravity boots back on. Then she climbed up on the winner's stand. Someone slipped a medal around her neck. No one seemed to notice that she was wearing gravity boots, although one of the contestants was staring at her. He had made the next highest jump and come in second. Kiki had heard he was on the Beta team.

Carlos pushed his way through the crowd. Kiki saw him and ran over.

"We have to get out of here," Carlos said. "I don't like the look that tall guy just gave you. We should get back to the ship. No one knows we came down here. Your dad may be looking for us."

Kiki shrugged. "Don't worry," she said. "No one knows who I am. We've got time. I haven't heard the ship's signal yet, have you? Dad knows I never go too far away, and the ship is just over the hill. This is just the best thing in the whole wide universe, isn't it? I'm having so much fun. I've never been good at sports, and now I'm a winner. What's the next event?"

"It's the ball toss," Carlos sighed. "You're not thinking of doing that one too, are you? We've got to get out of here."

Kiki could tell that Carlos wasn't very happy with her. She didn't care. She was a winner!

"Wow!" Kiki said. "Just think of it! On Earth I can't throw far at all. In weak gravity I'll be able to throw it to another galaxy."

"So will everyone else," Carlos grumbled.

"I'm used to throwing in stronger gravity," Kiki laughed. "Just you wait. I'll win this one for sure."

The announcer was saying, "We have four events, so get ready for the next one. Swish your tail, tell a tale, climb a stair, do not stare. We have some cool rules. They're not fool rules, or school rules, or pool rules. Everyone gets one turn to throw the ball. The person who throws it the farthest is the winner. That's all."

"This will be so easy," Kiki whispered to herself. "I'm a winner for sure."

Kiki was right. She had no trouble throwing the ball at all in Beta's weaker gravity. Her muscles were used to picking up and throwing balls that felt heavier in Earth's stronger gravity. She just picked up the ball and let it go. It zoomed above the trees and the clouds, and up, up, up into the suns' rays. She couldn't see where it came down.

No one had ever seen anything like it. They cheered and called her a hero. They ran over and patted her on the back. They asked where she learned how to throw a ball like that.

"Uh…well, I practiced a lot," she said.

The crowd cheered some more, and someone slipped another medal around her neck. She was a winner! She was the greatest! She was a star!

She ran over to Carlos and jumped up and down. "Isn't this amazing?" she cried. "Isn't this the best thing in the whole universe?"

Carlos wasn't laughing. He wasn't even smiling. He was not happy at all.

"You'll do anything to win," he said. Then he turned and walked away.

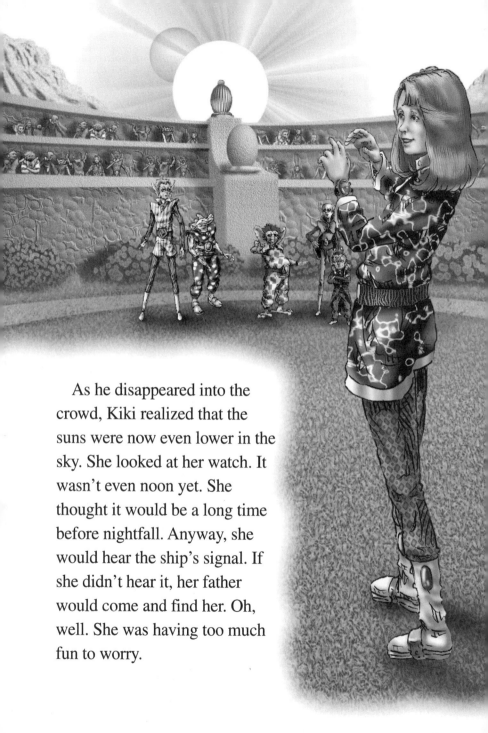

As he disappeared into the crowd, Kiki realized that the suns were now even lower in the sky. She looked at her watch. It wasn't even noon yet. She thought it would be a long time before nightfall. Anyway, she would hear the ship's signal. If she didn't hear it, her father would come and find her. Oh, well. She was having too much fun to worry.

CHAPTER 4

Win! Win! Win!

The announcer was telling about the next event. "Don't be late. We cannot wait. This is the third event. Not a lump or a bump, it's the long jump. We've got some cool rules. They're not school rules or fool rules or pool rules. Just jump as far as you can."

Kiki wondered whether she should wear her gravity boots for this event. The boots would keep her from jumping too high, but would she be able to jump very far? She had to think of a way that she could use gravity to jump farther than anyone else. She was determined to win. She was going to go back to Earth with a medal from each of the four events no matter what happened. This was her chance to prove that she was a winner.

Kiki thought about how to win the long jump while the others were lining up. She thought about it while the first contestant was jumping. She thought about it while the second contestant was jumping.

While the third contestant was jumping, she thought about Earth's moon. She remembered seeing a film of the first humans walking on the moon. As she thought about the film, she remembered seeing the astronaut Neil Armstrong hopping about. How long ago had that been? She did some fast math and came up with 528 years. Maybe he had been able to jump around on the moon because he was wearing gravity boots 528 years ago. She wasn't sure, as she had never read or seen anything that said the first Earth astronauts wore gravity boots. If Armstrong had worn gravity boots, they probably weren't as heavy as the boots she had on, Kiki thought.

That was it! If she took some of the padding and
metal plates out of her boots, she could jump far and
not too high. Quickly, she hid behind a bush. She took
some of the metal out of her boots. She stood up and
her feet stayed on the ground. She hopped and came
back down. She jumped ahead and landed perfectly.

Kiki raced to the pit just in time to do her jump. She could run very well with some of the metal out of her boots. In fact, she could race like the wind. After she finished the long jump, she wouldn't have any trouble with the 100-yard dash. She'd win that one for sure.

It was her turn, and everyone was watching. The people in the stands were cheering and shouting. They didn't know her name or what team she was on, so they yelled, "Come on, Squiggle Kid!"

She jumped. She went up just high enough and far enough, and came down perfectly.

She won! She had jumped farther than anyone else in the event. She had broken the record for the farthest long jump ever in the history of the Alpha Galaxy Games. She'd be in the Aggie Hall of Fame

Someone slipped another medal around her neck. Now she had three beautiful, heavy gold medals. She was such a star!

The crowd cheered, and she raised her arms above her head. Nothing like this had ever happened to her in her whole life. She was the star of these games, and it felt wonderful!

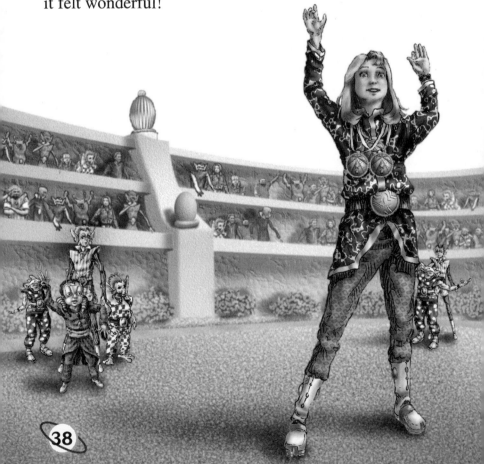

Suddenly, Kiki heard a voice behind her. She turned.
It was the very tall contestant.

"Hello, I'm Grymx from the planet Beta," the
contestant said, leaning down to speak to Kiki. The
words crackled in English from Kiki's translator watch.
Kiki smiled nervously.

"What planet did you say you're from?" Grymx
asked.

Kiki said quickly, "Zera. It's on the other side of the
galaxy, a long way from here."

"I don't think . . ." Grymx started to say.

"Listen," Kiki said quickly as she moved away from Grymx. "The announcer is talking about the last event."

Kiki ran onto the field. When she looked around, she noticed the sky was getting darker. The suns were beginning to set. Kiki looked at her watch again. It was just after noon. What was going on? she wondered. What was it that Carlos had said about Beta when they had first arrived? Kiki couldn't think about it for very long. It was time for the last event.

Then Kiki heard the announcer say, "Night is coming. We must hurry. It's time for the last event today. It's fun, so let's run until we are done. It's the 100-yard dash. It's not a smash, or a mash, or a crash. We've got some cool rules. They're not school rules or fool rules or pool rules. Just run as fast as you can."

Kiki headed for the starting line. She thought she heard some kind of horn in the distance. Then she thought she heard Carlos calling from the sidelines. It sounded as though he was saying, "The ship is about to go." She didn't want to stop to find out. She was having too much fun, and the race was about to begin.

As she took her place, she thought, What had the announcer meant when he said, "Night is coming. We must hurry"? Was it going to get dark already?

When the announcer said, "On your mark," Kiki heard another noise next to her. She glanced to the right and saw Grymx staring directly at her. Then his eyes shifted to Kiki's feet.

Just as the starting buzzer went off, Grymx yelled, "She's wearing some kind of gravity boots! She's not from the Alpha Galaxy." Kiki dashed off as fast as she could go.

CHAPTER 5
Caught in Midair

As she ran, Kiki thought about what Carlos had said. "You'll do anything to win," he had said. Maybe he was right. At this moment she really would do anything to have four medals to bring back to Earth and show all her friends.

Kiki glanced behind her as she ran. She was surprised to see race officials running after her as well as the other runners. Oh, no! she thought. They weren't just following her. They were chasing her.

Kiki could move very well after taking some of the metal out of her boots. She knew that she could run. She had run over to the long jump with these very same boots on. Now she had to run like the wind to get away from all the angry people that were running behind her.

As she ran, Kiki kept thinking what it would be like to have four medals around her neck. Four beautiful heavy gold medals would jiggle and shimmer when she walked around the halls of her school. Her friends would think she was very special. They would shake her hand and pat her on the back.

There was just one problem. Even if she crossed the finish line first, she probably wouldn't win this race if they knew she wasn't a real contestant. They might arrest her or something.

Kiki began to think that maybe three medals would be enough. Certainly her friends would admire her for three medals just as much as they would for four medals. Now would probably be a good time to get back to the ship.

Suddenly, she had a scary thought. The horn sound she had heard had been the ship! It was going to take off! It really was almost nightfall.

Kiki ran to the side of the track and started running for the trees. She thought if she could get behind them, she could circle back around and find Carlos. Then they could run up the hill in the same spot where they had first come down.

As she ran, she glanced behind her again. The crowd of people chasing her were much closer than they should have been. They were actually gaining on her. "STOP!" she heard someone yell.

Kiki wondered why she wasn't running as fast as she did when she ran to the long jump. Then she remembered. She had only been wearing two medals when she raced to the long jump pit. She had won that event, and they had given her another medal. The medals were heavy, and now she was wearing more weight than she had before. She was too heavy, and that's why she was slowing down. Kiki pulled off a medal and tossed it aside.

She kept running, but soon she realized she was slowing down even more. Maybe she should throw away another medal. Then she would have only one. There wasn't anything special about that. Lots of her friends on Earth had one medal. If she didn't throw it aside, though, those people behind her would catch her and she'd be in real trouble.

She pulled off a second medal and cast it onto the grass. She ran faster, then faster still. As she ran, she rose up in the air a little before she came down because now she was lighter.

Kiki looked up to make sure she was running in the right direction. She saw Carlos at the top of the hill. He was jumping up and down, and waving his arms. Was he yelling hurry, hurry?

She wondered what would happen if she tossed the last medal aside. Maybe she would sprint ahead and get to the hill before they caught her. She looked around and saw Grymx close behind her. Kiki pulled off the third medal and flung it into the grass.

Suddenly, Kiki felt long, strong fingers grabbing her shoulders. Then she was up in the air. Her feet were still moving, but they weren't on the ground. She turned her head and looked into the growling face of Grymx.

"There is no planet Zera in the Alpha Galaxy, is there?" Grymx growled. "You are not an Aggie contestant, so you're in a lot of trouble."

Kiki heard her voice squeak, trying to speak. Her mind raced with the thought that she would never see her father again, never see Carlos, never get back to her home planet, Earth.

Night Falls

Suddenly, it was dark. It was like a curtain coming down on a stage. In just a few seconds, the last of the light was gone. Kiki looked up. The last edges of both suns had dipped below the horizon.

Grymx gasped and dropped Kiki. "I've got to get inside," he said. Then he turned around and disappeared, running as fast as he could.

Kiki sat on the ground and rubbed her knee. She had bumped it hard when Grymx dropped her. What was wrong? she thought. Why had he run away just because it got dark?

She remembered now what Carlos had said when they had first arrived. He had said they didn't know what time it was on Beta or how long the day was. Then she remembered what the captain had said. Beta was smaller than Earth. It must also turn faster than Earth, Kiki thought. The days must be only about half as long as the days on Earth.

Then she remembered one more thing and was suddenly very scared. "The ship!" she said aloud. "The captain said the ship was supposed to leave before nightfall." It was now night.

Kiki moaned. What was she going to do? She knew her father wouldn't leave without her, but what if the captain didn't listen to him? Would they be stranded on Beta for good?

Kiki got up. Her knee was stiff and sore, but she didn't let that stop her. She started scrambling up the hill as fast as she could. She hoped she would get to the top and see the ship on the other side.

Suddenly, she fell into a crackling mass of stiff scratchy things. She was in the bushes she and Carlos had pushed through when they first came over the hill. The sticky leaves pulled at her clothes once more and slapped hard against her face and hands.

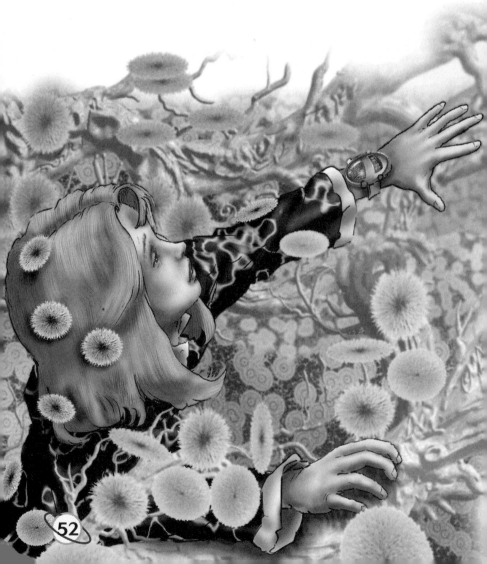

Kiki also realized it was quickly getting colder. She had another scary thought. Was that why Grymx ran away? Were the nights on Beta very cold? Would she freeze to death? She moaned again.

Suddenly she felt something grab her hand. Whatever it was held on and pulled her through the bushes. She screamed. Then a voice said, "Kiki, it's me. Don't scream."

"Carlos! Oh, I'm so glad it's you! Did the ship leave?" she gasped.

"No, your dad wouldn't let them. I told them where you were, but we couldn't get to you before it got dark. The captain is furious. He says if he waits much longer it will be too cold to take off," Carlos said.

"How are we going to find the ship?" Kiki asked. "It's so dark."

"If we can get to the top of the hill, we should be able to see the ship's lights," Carlos said.

"Wait a minute," Kiki said. "It seems to be getting a little lighter."

She was right. Now they could see the shapes of the bushes behind them. They both looked up. Low in the sky was a very small moon. Its light was weak, but maybe it was enough to show them the way to the top of the hill.

Kiki looked down the hill toward the arena. It was empty. Everyone had gone inside the building that was next to the arena. Then she caught sight of a dim glimmer on the ground. It was one of her medals. She had a quick thought. If she could see where she was going, it wouldn't take long to climb down and grab that medal and slip it around her neck. One medal from the Aggies was better than nothing.

"Oh, no!" Carlos said. He had seen Kiki look down the hill. He had seen the shiny medal, too. "We have to get back to the ship. You don't need that medal, Kiki."

"But . . ." Kiki started to say. Carlos didn't listen to another word. He just grabbed her hand and started pulling her toward the top of the hill.

At the top, they stopped to catch their breath and see where the ship was. They could see it in the distance. The bright lights were a welcome sight. What was not such a welcome sight was that the ship was rising off the ground.

"They're taking off!" Kiki cried.

CHAPTER 7
Leaving Beta

Carlos and Kiki started down the hill, trying to run. They couldn't go very fast, though, because they were feeling colder and colder. At the bottom of the hill, they had slowed to a walk.

"Faster," Carlos panted.

"I can't go any faster," Kiki cried. "I'm so cold. My legs feel like blocks of ice."

"Kiki, come on," Carlos pleaded. "We've got to keep going."

"What's the use?" Kiki cried. "The ship has taken off without us." She slumped to the ground.

"No, it hasn't," Carlos said. "I know they won't leave without us." He was worried, though. What if she was right? He stared at the ship as it rose and seemed to move away from them.

Suddenly the ship began to turn. It was headed back toward Kiki and Carlos.

"Kiki, look!" Carlos cried. He pulled her up and pointed to the sky.

"How will they ever find us?" Kiki said. "It's still too dark to find us." Her voice was shaking. Carlos wasn't sure if it was excitement, fear, or the cold.

Kiki's question was answered almost immediately. Large, bright spotlights lit up the bottom of the spaceship. They cast a glowing circle on the ground.

Kiki and Carlos stumbled toward the circle of light. When they entered it, a hatch opened in the bottom of the ship. A two-person seat was lowered. Kiki and Carlos climbed in and were lifted into the spaceship.

Inside the ship, Kiki's father ran to her. Kiki hugged him and cried. "I'm so sorry, Dad," she sobbed. "I never meant for this to happen. I was so excited about the games, I just didn't think."

"You and Carlos are all right," Kiki's dad said. "That is what's important now. We'll talk later."

Carlos and Kiki took their seats. They were very tired. "So how do you feel now about being in the Alpha Galaxy Games?" Carlos asked.

"It was a dumb thing to do," Kiki told him. "You were right, Carlos. I didn't think about what I was doing because I was having so much fun. All I wanted to do was win, and that's not right. I put you and this whole ship in danger. If I'm ever going to be a winner, I've got to do it fairly. If I never win, well, that's OK too. I don't need a medal to feel special."

Carlos smiled at her. He was almost asleep. Kiki turned and looked out the window. Her medals were lying somewhere in the grass, but it was too dark for her to see them. Outside the window, the night was as black as a crow's feather.

"I'd rather just be myself, winner or not. That's what's important," Kiki said. She looked out at the hundreds of faraway stars twinkling in the distance. One of them was her own sun. She would be glad to get home. This new year would be very special. Kiki had learned something about herself and it felt good.

Glossary

arena [uh REE nuh] a space surrounded by seats in which contests are held

cast [kast] throw or let fall

contestants [kun TES tunts] people who take part in a contest or trial of skill, such as a game or a race

extreme [ek STREEM] much more than usual; very great or strong

furious [FYOOR ee us] full of wild anger

gravity [GRA vuh tee] the force that causes things to have weight and that holds things onto Earth

lurched [lurcht] a sudden leaning or rolling to one side

officials [uh FIH shuls] people who are in charge of something

rhythmic [RITH-mik] having a motion or sound that happens in a regular pattern or beat

translator [TRANZ lay tor] a person or object that changes one language into another